Lost & Found:
Poems Found All Around

Greg Zeck

Dead White Man Press
Fayetteville, Arkansas
2021

Copyright © 2021 by Gregory R. Zeck

ISBN 978-1-7356161-1-7

Library of Congress Control Number 2021942538

Manufactured in the United States of America

Cover art of glove puppet with permission of Judy McSween Paintings LLC

Typeset in 11-point Sitka Text and other Sitka styles

For Mom & Dad
(Mary M. Zeck, 1915-1991,
and Robert E. Zeck, 1913-2008),
without whom, as they say, where would we be?

> Lost is lost and found is found
> Around the corner silent peeking.
> Turn the tables round and round.
> Show me that which I am seeking.
> — *Spell to Find a Lost Object*[1]

---

[1] This is the only footnote you will find in the volume, but the copious endnotes on pp. 111-127 offer origins, explanations, divagations, and extravagances for most of the poems that may or may not help you appreciate them.

FOREWORD
A Few Words on the Genesis & Evolution of These Poems

I can't recall just when I started finding these poems, or how the poems found me. What were the sources, that is, and resources? How did I come to think of these sources as poetry or poetic possibility?

In the largest sense, I came to realize, a poem can be found, as the subtitle of this volume suggests, "all around." If we are open, or receptive, to language in its multifarious guises, we can't help but be astonished by what happens when mouths are opened, pens picked up, and the babbling begins. If language is purely a transactive medium, of course, an exchange of this bit of information for that bit, we might not feel wonder in the exchange. But if we vibrate with the rhythmic suggestions of language — its intricacies, subtleties, marvels, ludicrosities — then how can we help but be amazed and astonished?

Words are all around us. They're the cultural and biological soup in which we live and swim. They're in our heads and mouths, our songs, ads, newspapers, books, obits. They're inescapable. They drive us mad and enable us to be suave, making life on earth with others of our ornery species possible and possibly dangerous.

If we are readers, habitual processors of the written word, we are often astonished by reading stuff that's not simply transactional (manuals, receipts, requests, scientific reports) but blows us off our comfy reading seats as if we'd just taken a cannon shot to the belly or the brain. Some of the poems in this volume began for me as this kind of experience of ordnance. I think of the often violent and always passionate stories in Svetlana Alexievich's *Secondhand Time: The Last of*

FOREWORD

the Soviets (1995), a Dostoevskian account via oral interviews of Russian suffering in the Great Patriotic War (WW II) and Stalinist purges to various post-war Soviet leaders. (See Part 7, "When We Have Fears that We May Cease to Be," pp. 86-90.)

Alexievich's stories make us almost ashamed to be leading comfortable bourgeois existences, unthoughtful and uneventful by comparison to Russian lives. But they give us vicarious access to the dramas and sufferings of those who witness and undergo these events.

Finding the source of a found poem is one thing. Then knowing or learning what to do with it, how to marshal creative resources, is something else. On the technical level, it seems to me, selection and syntax are the chief criteria for turning a source into a poem — something else if not something else entirely, a bit of language set aside and displayed on its own as if it were a jewel or geode or intimate portrait. Like any artist, the poet has to know what goes in and what stays out. (Sometimes a great deal stays in a found poem, and the poet need add few words of his own. Sometimes the opposite, as in poems that depend on only a phrase or sentence, not an entire situation.) The poet must deploy the tidbit he overhears or overreads in a context where it makes sense on its own, and must control the length and pulse of the sentence and stanza, the rhythm of the entire piece.

In short, when sources are found, they are animated and apprised almost instantly as poetry or poetic possibility. They are lifted from their sources, put in a new frame or context, something set apart, something not necessarily precious but often astonishing. Not all found poems are dramatic or violent, of course, but if you look at them in the light of your comfy reading lamp and daily experience, they can sometimes lift you up or knock you off your seat.

Happy reading, then, whether you're sitting pretty or already on the edge of your chair.

Greg Zeck
Fayetteville, Arkansas
October 2021

P.S. In the 5/27/2021 *New York Review of Books,* the musician Julian Hemphill, "a blues surrealist," is portrayed as one who borrowed sources "without permission," including the words of his hero Ralph Ellison. Ellison's wife assured Hemphill, "You can have [the work] as long as you don't make any money off it." Like Hemphill, I assure you that poets too may pilfer but rarely profit financially.

TABLE OF CONTENTS

1. Words, Words, Words
Frame 3
How to Write a Found Poem 4
Poem in Form of To-do List... 5
Sackcloth 6
Nothing 7
Dung Beetle 8
Rhyme Time 9
Language 10
Reverie 11
Myopia: Word of the Day 12
Orchidaceous: Word of the Day.. 13
Poem Constructed of Words of the Day............................. 14

2. Song & Dance
Bist Du bei Mir 17
Jazz Allegro 18
Miller's Tale 19
Poem I've Been Hoarding in a Drawer 20
Tempus Fugit 21
What We're Looking For 22
Refugees 24
April Fool's Day Hike 26
Waldeinsamkeit 27

3. Capitalism & Its Discontents
Men's Health 31
Enlarge Your Penis Now 32
Pahokee, Florida 33
Poem in Two Faces and Seven Fonts 34
James Patterson Teaches How to Write a Best-selling Novel 35
Out of Sorts and Out of Work 36
Principal Life 37
Birdbath: Product Review 38
Brassiere: Product Review 39

Matsu El Recio: Wine Review 40
In Praise of Pinot Blanc: Wine Review................................. 41
New World Winner: Wine Review 42
Search Me: LinkedIn 43
Things to Do in Evening Shade, Arkansas 44

4. News of the Day
Supply Chain Resilience 47
Tremors 48
Blurred Borders 49
Base Jump 50
Accidental Elegy 52
Man Charged in Death of Man Found in River.................... 53

5. Politics & the Polity
Seattle Climate Report... 57
Gun Control 58
Required Reading for Those Who Will Not Read 60
Homicide Stenographer Rant 62
Supreme Court Rejects Trump's Bid to Shield Tax Returns .. 63
Otto Warmbier: 1994–2017 64
New York City Climate Report.. 65

6. Stories Remembered & Invented
The Cypriot Way 69
Face 1: Catholic School 70
Face 2: Social Media 72
Chex 73
Hot Thai Dinner chez Zeck 74
Things Our Father Used to Say 75
The Sensitive Zeck Boys 76
Soul 77

7. When We Have Fears that We May Cease to Be
Fort Riley, Kansas 83
To the Sterile Sedge 84
Dunes 85

Beautiful Bitches 86
The Executioner 87
Shit Bucket 88
Tenderness...89
War 90

8. Messages from the Living & the Dead
Honest Apology from Christian Girl and Reply 93
How Are Things Moving 94
Poem for My Brother in His Own Words 95
The Void 96
Squalor..98
Barbara 100
Robert Goad, 1947–2020...101
Thomas B. Whitbread, 1931–2016 102
Martin Dworkin, 1927–2014 103
Randall Lankford, 1943–2020 104
On Buzzard's Wings 105
How Not to Write an Obituary 106
I've Said All I Have to Say 108

Endnotes
Endnotes 111

Graphics
Graphics 128

Biography
Greg Zeck 129

x

1. WORDS, WORDS, WORDS

Frame
By way of epigraph

I put a frame around it
so I can say I found it,
so I can say it's yours and mine
for this brief space of time.

WORDS, WORDS, WORDS

How to Write a Found Poem

Think of it as collage, from French *colle* paste,
glue (<Greek *kólla*) + *-age,* as in mucilage, I'd add,
Middle English *muscilage* <Middle French *musillage*
<Late Latin *mūcilāgō* a musty juice, akin to *mūcēre*
to be musty. Also see *mucor* if you must. But where
were we? Oh, yes, *collage* and *mucilage.* I'm glad you
asked. To write a found poem look for it in the stuff
of every day, the natural or not, who cares, language
of men and women as they work and play and carry
on in newspaper comments, for example, want ads
personal or not, oral interviews, social media, old
letters, obits, the blab of the pave perhaps, a story
heard or overheard, an event, a quote that hangs
in the air, the dictionary too, the historical repository
of our yearnings and wanderings, and then fix your
attention on the fresh phrase, throw out the chaff,
seize the good stuff in your beak, jackdaw or jill,
don't hold back, what are you thinking?
There's so much of it, and all so tasty.

Poem in Form of To-do List

- Finish Claudia's website
- Wash summer clothes
- Practice Gregg shorthand
- Organize your 9 lives on hard drives
- Buy 6-volt lantern for camping and tornadoes
- Tell Jen you love her
- Drive Mom to the Beauty Barn (if Mom were only here)
- Snap pix of armadillos DOR (you're not in Minnesota anymore)
- Tell Diana how much you care
- Study Djokovic's lethal backhand
- Tell Tom he's a no-good dirty bastard
- Plan family reunion
- Ask Jen what she meant by the child that died
- Help in kitchen (only if she asks)
- Meditate on where you've been and where the hell you're going

WORDS, WORDS, WORDS

Sackcloth
To Bembo, whose wife and mine too look with disdain on our dishabille

It's not that either you
or I, sir, give two hoots
in hell about the clothing
we wear on our backs
or behinds, but sackcloth,
sir? You say sackcloth?

Why not say sailcloth,
the way we bardlings,
along for the ride, fly
with Apollo and his steeds
through gold or silver sky?

Ashes, sir? You insist
on ashes? Eventually,
sodden truth for sure,
we all fall down. Our
soigné old ladies too
come tumbling after.

Nothing

"Nothing seems to be right anymore. Everything tastes a little waxy." — Bembo making moan

After a visit to the dentist, friend,
consider the bitter truths of the ancients:
how our taste buds mutiny, our teeth
grow long, and the globed fruit
of our being, about which our
pal Archie discourses, sticks
out the calyx of its tongue
and talks back. Oh for the
days of mute regressive glory!
We look back, poking our tongue
into memory's corner, reconnoitering
the moments when everything we probed
tasted good, so good, our dinners exquisite,
our thoughts divine, our old ladies young ladies,
and we ourselves bursting into bloom. Ahem.
Your attention, please, one moment, you old dozer.
Your forbearance, if you would, whilst I extract the wax
from my hairy ear. What exactly is it you were saying?

WORDS, WORDS, WORDS

Dung Beetle
Daily drivel with Gerry Sloan

X: So when you coming down off the mountain?
Y: Too rainy now, plus the missy has been pissy.
X. Pissy missy will not let you go? Pissy missy love you so? Then pissy missy isn't pissy, is she?
Y: Some days you're the pigeon, some days the statue.
X: You can shit your own head as well as pants?
Y: Done it, but don't recommend.
X: There's a poem for you somewhere.
Y: Caca chapbook?
X: Whole lotta shit hitting the poetic fan.
Y: The story of my life.
X: Be a dung beetle and roll with it.
Y: Good T-shirt slogan.
X. Good Facebook logon.
Y. Make poetry pay.
X: Watched *Tiny World,* the other night — a dung beetle rolling elephant shit up Sisyphean rills and ruts. What courage! What panache!
Y: The female chooses the male with the biggest ball of shit?
X: The biggest ball of poetry!

Rhyme Time
Perusing the rhyming dictionary, the poet sends forth celeritous seed

For starts, how about hilarity?
Make that guffaw.
Vulgarity?
Enough of that stuff you've stuffed in your craw.
Spontaneity?
Sure, if you've had time to prepare.
Velleity?
Who wouldn't wish it, ever so lightly?
Temerity?
Clap on your breastplate, sirrah dog!
Timidity?
Gorgeous amaryllis, shy timothy.
Reactionary?
You must be thinking MAGA.
Apothecary?
These days they carry also wine and dairy.
Bestiary?
Rise up from your muddy rut, you animal!
Quaternary?
The fourth from the top.
Tertiary?
The third, you feckless fop.
Secondary?
To none, if you are lucky.
Primary?
Cock o' the walk!
Temporary?
Run, don't walk!
Celerity?
Godspeed to you, sir, and your pokey fertility.

WORDS, WORDS, WORDS

Language
In the voice of Samanta Schweblin

Gravid, rigid, inexact, orality
has always made me uncomfortable.
Consider how easy it is to open the mouth

and say something that afterward we'd rather
not have said, how terrifying to name out loud
this thing that hasn't been said and now it's

something real: angry, irrevocable action,
reaction, whirlwinds provoked by words.
This is why I would rather give up speaking,

you see, and stick to putting down on the page
one word after the other, choosing carefully,
eschewing the noises and dangers of speaking,

so stopping the cacophony of the stupidly merry
go round, giving me the time I need to say exactly
what I want to say to master this little world.

Reverie
For Jennifer

Dawnhead flashes *improbable ground
of essence.* Then thunder. Then leap
from bed to computer only to find
philosophical twaddle: Aristotle
and his *to ti en einai* (*Metaphysics,* VII, 7),
that whereby a thing is what it is,
fundamental ground of the soul,
whatever the soul is and who knows?

Return to bedrock, then, wife's soft
round rump rising with her breathing:
content, for the time being, all we have:
pull duvet up, pat ground of essence softly,
softly murmuring *love, love, love.*

WORDS, WORDS, WORDS

Myopia: Word of the Day
For Jen again

You say you can't see anything beyond
the tip of your nose, my love, yet if this is
myopia it may owe, after all, to the Greek
myōpía, nearsightedness, i.e. (*id est*),
to use a Latinism, something contagious
and coming down to you, honestly enough,
through the obscure centuries, deriving
from *mýein,* to close the eyes or mouth
(close kin to the Latin *mūtus,* inarticulate,
dumb, silent, or, as we'd say in English,
mute, which, true enough, sweetheart,
you have seldom been). Consider too *mystikós,*
connected with the mysteries or mystic,
an enchanted Greek isle perhaps? And let's
not forget *-ōpía,* a combining form of *ṓps*
(stem *ōp-*), meaning eye, face, countenance,
and the gods know yours are beautiful: *opa!*
For what doth it profit a man, or woman,
to gain the entire world if he/she closes
the eyes, or mouth, and trips over the obvious,
a metaphorical sense, inability or unwillingness
to act prudently, developed in English only
at the hyperopic end of the 19th century.
So look, look, look, my true love, and see.
Here we are then, you and me, together
this blazing instant. Let that be a lesson.

Orchidaceous: Word of the Day
For Jen, who else?

How do I love thee? Let me count a way.
Thou art more orchidaceous than an orchid,
which is obvious, which is to say not ghostly,
for gods' sakes, you so vibrantly alive, your
flesh opening sesame, quivering or quiet or
modest, though you have little cause, darling,
to be modest or merely drably interesting.

When we met, after all, how many years ago,
you came out not a debutante, or flame, or
fragrance, though you were all of these, but
flower (to be specific, terrestrial or epiphytic
plant of the Orchidaceae family, of temperate
and tropical regions, having showy flowers),
and you're showing me even now, my lady, how
many incredible years later, and I'm telling you
here and now, my love, in the blooming moment,
my love is pure grateful astonishment.

WORDS, WORDS, WORDS

Poem Constructed of Words of the Day

We have spoken of the annoying tendency to **pleonasm** in Lucian's style, which must be laid at the door of rhetoric. Human feelings, it is true, are the same everywhere, but we have more of the artificial and *factitious* in us than we are aware of. As for ***ply,*** a more or less familiar word, it can mean: make repairs, renovations, revisions or adjustments to; apply oneself diligently; speak or utter in a certain way; collect or gather. Are not those palsies and apoplexies more dangerous which commence many days before the ***syzygies*** of the moon than those which happen when three celestial bodies are configured in a line? There were narrow passages down which tortured men must once have been carried, or at the end of which some ***oubliette*** or other opened to sudden destruction. On the lower row are interlacing semicircles in high relief, each of which forms a ***cusp*** and is painted blue. Where would you, Inspector Clouseau, most likely find a ***cordon?*** In a voice of suppressed rage I said a thing that brought the slender little ***virago*** at once to reason. The city planners, of course, have no monopoly on ***prescience*** despite their use of graphs, maps, and statistics to ***limn*** the future, wouldn't you agree?

2. SONG & DANCE

Bist Du bei Mir
After J. S. Bach for J. S. Zeck

Bist du bei mir sang the soloist at our
wedding when we hitched our sexy
wagons to each other's star. *Geh' ich
mit Freuden,* she descanted, I'll go
with joy, *Bübchen* or *Mädchen,* as long
as you're with me. We'd met in German
class at the U, where we learned that *Bach*
meant brook and my mother's maiden name
Bachler one who dwells by the brook,
your maiden name *Saltzman* salt man,
salt of the earth, but if the salt were to lose
its savor, my tasty dish, wherewith would it
be salted, your father performing the wedding
to have and to hold at the seven-bedroom lake
lodge he'd restored for all his dainty daughters.
As long as you both shall live and you're with me,
I'll gladly go to death and to my rest, *zum Sterben
und zu meiner Ruh'. Ach, wie vergnügt,* can you
imagine the pleasure it would give were you,
and you alone, *wär so mein Ende,* to be the one
at the very end, you and your drop dead gorgeous
hands, slim and true and tapering into flame,
to be there finally, *drückten deine schönen Hände,*
my true love, my heart's desire, *mir die getreuen
Augen zu,* to close my eyes, my true eyes finally, forever.

SONG & DANCE

Jazz Allegro
With a nod o the beret to John Milton

Scat, sad cat, Mistah Penseroso,
an take yo black coffee witchoo
an yo black crow. It long bout
midnight now, an this heah set
bout ovah. This heah cat don
mean to rise an shine an slave
tomorrow nine to five fo Mastah
Cromwell. An take that damn crow
witchoo: cheeky scavenger ain't
no rapta, hawk, or eagle. Send
in that cheerful chick Euphrosyne,
who kin hep herself to a toot or two
o ma fine bottle o Courvoisier,
Ms. Eye Candy in spades, no shit —
buxom, blithe, and debonair —
hot damn, yeah! an them snaky
tresses fallin to er booty.

Miller's Tale
With apologies to Geoffrey Chaucer

I pray for her.
She preys on me.
Perfect equanimity.

I'm invisible.
What's the *jeune fille* see in me?
Diamonds forever, dollars almighty?

And what at last do I see in her
besides great legs and ass
and superstructural gun rack?

I long for her
as the lambkin for the teat
et le mouvement anti-psychiatrique.

SONG & DANCE

Poem I've Been Hoarding in a Drawer
Thinking of Frank O'Hara

Sure, socks, tees, and bikini briefs cohabit
in this fine and private place, grave of a sere
and obscure drawer. And when scraps of poetry
also, stray spraints or scats, pack of street mutts,
anoesis of barks, sniffs, scratches, are found here
one day, after I am gone, stuff I hid away, a dusty
cluster of what might have been, and perhaps was,
back in the day: okay, okay, okay.

Tempus Fugit
For Pam and Mike

Tempus fugit. Fuck it.
I'm having fun,
the doddering, drooling
old fool that I am.

SONG & DANCE

What We're Looking For
The editors of little literary magazines scratch the dirt for the right words

We're searching for poetry that conveys in its composition — as well as in the sound, cadence, and possibly even musicality of its words — an expression of honesty and purpose that somehow rings true.

We want the vicious, the clinical, the confessional. We yearn for poems that cut from where the ache is still tender, and rend longing wide open. Pulling knives from the body to call them holy, crushing berries in fists like deliverance — we're looking for words that ask hunger what it's made of; works that spit blood on the floor every time they try to speak.

We want earnest and diverse work that is brave, illuminating, and emotionally detailed and that can be celebrated on the same page as sophisticated design.

We are interested in works that destabilize the subject/object binary in an embattled cultural environment where the line between fiction and non-fiction blurs with each passing news cycle.

We seek mysteries and marginalized voices, a sense of shared wonder, inclusive art that asks questions, explores mystery, and works to make visible the marginalized, the overlooked, and those whose voices have been silenced, including LGBTQ+, neurodivergent writers, women and women writers.

We earnestly solicit work about economic decline and race riots. Work about disability or by disabled writers. Work by writers fifty years old or older. The resource poor, whether urban or rural.

Those who have experienced incarceration. Work about the nonhuman, or work that challenges anthropocentrism.
We want work that grows in complexity upon each visitation; we enjoy ornate, cerebral, and voluptuous prose executed with thematic intent.

We publish nothing but the truest ethos of the current times — the quintessential yet varied, fast-diversifying yet emblematic "spirit," so to speak, of the exciting, post-modernist times we are living in.

SONG & DANCE

Refugees
Inspired by Bao Phi's "Adrift"

No longer refugees, nothing to flee from,
we dream the voyage over once again —
strange customs, multiple humiliations
in a tongue we cannot speak, the babble
we must process to make ourselves
personae gratae here in others' eyes.

We sail from Gdańsk or Danzig, say,
who owns the place anyway,
with our family of Polish peasants,
fresh off the potato-picking flatlands
of the south, it's 1870, post–American
Civil War, but what is that to us? We've
had our own centuries of servitude,
partition, patriotism, Catholicism.
In steerage, of course, crowded two
to four per bunk, we're slammed side
to side, off course, the seas heaving,
dysentery and typhoid rampant, and when
we land in Galveston, Texas, which might
as well be the moon, we take our first small
steps for man in the new world, our giant
steps we like to think for mankind, even as
we're shunted through customs like cows, like
the farmers we are, by God, whom we invoke
as he is in heaven, *któryś jest w niebie, święć
się imię twoje,* hallowed be his name, straitened
as we are by heart, soul, and bowed back, rural
priests, lords, sorcerers, and somehow even now
straightening up before we know it.

LOST & FOUND

Dirt poor, prodded like cattle, lumbering
off the ship, speaking our own tongue free
of vowels, a field of spiked grasses, snakes,
hornets, through customs strange to us
and rich, a language we will learn eventually
and use successfully, finding our place on farm
and church first, changing our names, becoming
Americans, moving to the city and its libraries
and universities and towers.

SONG & DANCE

April Fool's Day Hike

Here come ole Flattop, he be slidin, no foolin,
long ridge, steep holler, wildlife, wildflower,
trout lily, spring violet, crows and raccoons:
he got hair down to his knees, ain't lookin
round much, ain't too hard to please.

Now ticks be comin with they joojoo eyeballs,
with they legs extendin, mouths bitin groin:
give 'im alpha gal syndrome! can't eat no groun roun!
come together, can't you feel his disease,
come and shoot him please.

Waldeinsamskeit

Lost in the woods toward dusk
and finding only the old Romantic
Waldeinsamkeit, the oneness with the
woods and nature's beauty, sure, but let's
get real, the loneliness and terror too. *Hansel
und Gretel* and other texts read back in school,
*Die wilden Tiere würden bald kommen und sie
zerreißen,* the wild animals would soon come and
rip them apart, without getting lost in the guttural
thicket, tutored gently along the well-trod path of high
school and university. Yes, for every flower there was a
danger, for every child a witch. Lost in the woods now, though
not far from civilization and its discontents, *das Unbehagen in der
Kultur,* Herr Freud would say, the eerie discomfort in the midst
of all our comforts, only two mud bikers, one hiker with her
dog (she pink, he fluffy white), and one trail runner (what
are you thinking, fleeting youth, far too fast on a gloomy
day like this and young).

Stumbling in the woods, four hours and the dusk
coming on, a fine rain too, all semblance of things
known and loved receding: when suddenly blue phlox,
white dogwood, gold daffodils, booming choruses of spring
peepers and indeterminate birds up in the shortleaf pines making
a godawful racket: well, okay, not altogether lost but feeling more
than a little lonely and frankly scared as hell.

3. CAPITALISM & ITS DISCONTENTS

Men's Health
From the magazine of the same name

How can I express sufficient gratitude
for your March issue, which reveals,
once and for all, the answers to the life
questions I have been asking, vainly,
for years and years: How to Melt My
Man Boobs, How to Leave Her Moaning
for More, and, best of all, How to Tell
the Grim Reaper to Go to Hell. I'm going
to Man Up, for sure, Kick Ass When
Surrounded by Bullies, Lose 20 Pounds
in 4 Short Weeks, and Last Longer in Bed.
I might have to give up poetry for a while,
but what the hell, isn't poetry for sissies?

CAPITALISM & ITS DISCONTENTS

Enlarge Your Penis Now

Just listen to what women have to say about penis size. What solution is best for you, or solid or gas? Ron Jeremy reviews every top male enlargement pill. How to do it naturally with Colgate and Vaseline. Does it really work, you wonder wanker? Costs, risks, overall effectiveness. Jelq in the comfort of your own hand and home. Five proven steps. Love at first glans. The truth about pills and pumps. How to get the old blood up. Seven good hand exercises. Eeny weeny miny mo, catch a dick by the cameltoe. Augmentation is salvation. Don't leave your testicles behind. Vitamins will increase effects of stretching exercises. Cock rings, anyone? The beautiful truth you need to hear. Length and girth are gifts from the gods and for the girls. The rare truth and nothing but the truth, so help me gods. I am a female health doctor specializing in providing the penis health services that will drive women mad, including sufficient protein nutrients. Ten thick inches to astound your friends and confound your enemies. Sex is a gift of mother nature, motherfucker. Believe me, you should apply toothpaste to your dong and rub it in well. You will have earned that glazed look in her eyes. Here's the buzz, boys: a bee sting can produce permanent penis enlargement, no shit!

Pahokee, Florida

I don't know anyone in Pahokee,
Florida, so why are you calling me,
Pahokee? I don't know anyone named
Services. If I needed services, wouldn't
I call you? You call this a courtesy call,
do you, holding me upside down and
shaking the shekels from my pocket?

It's a far too gorgeous day for anyone
to be locked in a call center somewhere
the sun don't shine like Podunk Pahokee,
babbling crappy scripts. C'mon, man, take
that job and shove it and the corporation too.
Be human, man, all too human. Avoid doubt,
debt, and desperation. Let's take a hike now,
you and me, man, this very moment, c'mon,
into the sublimating sun.

CAPITALISM & ITS DISCONTENTS

Poem in Two Faces and Seven Fonts

As my lawyer father Mr. Merriweather Light was wont to say, once
    upon a time and far away, tapping his antique Smith Corona:
Now is the time for all good men to come to the aid of their party.

When I questioned the utility of said party, Mr. Merriweather
    Normal would look askance and down on me and say:
Now is the time for all good men to come to the aid of their party.

**When I looked up anguished at his legalistic visage, lined with
    years of service to the party, Mr. Merriweather Bold tapped:
Now is the time for all good men to come to the aid of their party.**

```
The anguish of the son, looking up at the father, Mr. Inconsolata
   Light, is hardly to be expressed in the words he typed:
Now is the time for all good men to come to the aid of their
   party.

The anguish and the wanting to look up and be looked up to, even
   as I watched the old pater, Mr. Inconsolata Normal,
   hunchbacked and blind, tapping out at his desk:
Now is the time for all good men to come to the aid of their
   party.

The anguish of becoming one's own father at last, like sweet milk
   curdling in a can, Mr. Inconsolata Semibold, soliloquizing to
   the setting sun:
Now is the time for all good men to come to the aid of their
   party.

Repeating with parched lips and parched brain the old and
   wearisome refrain, Mr. Inconsolata Bold:
Now is the time for all good men to come to the aid of
   their party.
```

James Patterson Teaches How to Write a Best-selling Novel

For the first time ever,
this old man with the caved
in face will teach you how to
write a bestseller. A mere ninety
bucks will put you too in touch not
with your feelings, who said anything
about your stupid feelings, but the pullulating
masses yearning to be free and meanwhile shelling
out their ten, twelve bucks at the grocery checkout or
airport bookstore for such dreck. Here's the deal: Lesson 1:
Passion + Habit. Lesson 2: Tricks of the Trade. Lesson 3: Raw
Ideas. Does it matter a scribbler's damn that James Patterson
does not write James Patterson anymore but has a stableful
of raw and bleeding mules just like you, Bucky? Raw ideas,
I say, not raw deal. Send in your measly ninety bucks
today, Becky. You get the drift.

CAPITALISM & ITS DISCONTENTS

Out of Sorts and Out of Work

Out of sorts and out of work I see
a want ad proclaiming the need for
a Failure Analysis Technician. By god,
I have some experience there. Let me

work up and burnish my experience
in failure, and brooding, and analyzing
same. It's a game I play with my head
nearly every day, and it's been a rewarding

career, make that careen, to date, though not
strictly monetarily. It has kept me off the streets,
I mean, and out of pulpits and radioactive labs
and sewers if not classrooms. It has schooled

me in the art of kicking myself in the head,
musing miserably, and writing reams of wretched
poetry that will not scan in HR. Time to shut up
already, then, and dust off the resume.

Principal Life

If you died tomorrow,
God forbid, says my friend,
the insurance agent provocateur,
if there is a God, it's his guess as good as
mine, forbid that you should die tomorrow,
that is. The day after tomorrow might be more
convenient, I reply. Tomorrow, you see, is fully booked,
I have events up the ying-yang starting with my morning
coffee with the boys, and as for today I'm afraid the calendar
is already chock-full. Damned if I wouldn't have a helluva
time finding time today to pay down even that measly
one dollar on the one-hundred-thousand-dollar life
insurance policy. God forbid indeed such a thing
should happen to a mere mortal man. Can't
Principal just mind its own business today?

CAPITALISM & ITS DISCONTENTS

Birdbath: Product Review

This solar birdbath is extremly well
packaged to protect every single componet,
to the frogs, the basin, pedistal ect. Very easy
to put together. The frogs eyes are so expressive,
I love the cattail details. The fountain inmeddiately
comes to life as sunlight hits the solar panel.
I love sitting on my patio listening to it
tricle as the wind blows my wind chime
and birds twitter. It makes me relax,
puts me in a good mood.

Brassiere: Product Review

This brassiere or Busenhälter (booby holder),
as we Germans like to say, folds up many times
unless you weigh 100 lbs. which is to say about
62 kilos and have no body fat like who is that?
Very excited to try this model for larger chested
ladies like me who need to shake it out and still
keep it contained. I could sleep in this bra or barge
down the Nile like Cleopatra. The most comfy bra
I own and the only one I ever want to wear if I
want to wear any. The material is like wearing
nothing it's so soft. Keeps boobs in place and no
spillage. Gave up on underwire years ago, no
wonder. Beyond thrilled with this bra. I am 36G
and, all things considered, this bra is great
for massive jugs. I wear this bra everywhere,
public and private, it's supportive, comfy, and I'm
38DD, what do you think of that? When I first put
this bra on I was quite surprised it fit my 34DDD
boobies perfectly. When you are blessed up top,
you know what I mean, you cannot go long
without support. Support is adequate but not
optimal. This may not be a good choice for very
large breasted women but men probably won't
mind. As it is, it is very comfortable and good
enough for wearing around the house, working
from home, quick errands, etc. Definitely
wouldn't wear it jogging, though, again,
men probably wouldn't mind.

CAPITALISM & ITS DISCONTENTS

Matsu El Recio: Wine Review

This tempranillo undergoes fourteen months
of malolactic fermentation in French oak barrels.
Corpulent and chewy, it has tons of finesse,
an intense nose with notes of chocolate, black
fruits, and vanilla. Mouthfeel is predominantly
round and silky, unctuous with subtle hints
of glycerine. Touches of fruits and minerals
linger in the aftertaste. Full bodied and easy
to drink alone or with others. 90 points, buy now.

In Praise of Pinot Blanc: Wine Review

The consummate food wine, it's a bit shy on the nose with lots of polleny floral tones, including almond, honeycomb, dried pear and peach; a gentle green herb spice note; the dice of river stone minerals; and, finally, a lovely bitter apple peel finish. Rated 92, drink now.

CAPITALISM & ITS DISCONTENTS

New World Winner: Wine Review

Pungent, weedy, and smoky,
at first it smells lean, Old
World, cool climate. Yet air
it, and the nose gains fruit
and focus. In the mouth, it's
ripe and complex, styled with
lots of bright red cherry fruit,
stiff little tannins, and juicy
acids for the dinner table.

There's a bit of cocoa on
the back end and the finish is
long with an earthy character
plus vanilla and spice tones
from the barrel. It's a little
rustic and tough at times
without the flamboyance or
opulence of most California
Merlots, but therein lies its
beauty. A lovely, expressive,
distinctive wine that one
can drink all night long
(but probably shouldn't)
and never tire of. 91 points.

Search Me: LinkedIn

This week I appeared in just one search.
I was not searching, was I? My design
in life, now that I am retired, is to be as
searchless if not clueless as possible, as
obscure as necessary for salivation if not
salvation, a very curious idea, don't you
think, and mysteriously incorporeal,
a throwback to ancient rites and the piety
of my youth, could be, which perhaps like
you too after many vain prayers I threw
away in various lewd and unprofitable
enterprises that cannot be searched,
thank gods, in any online database I know
of or mentioned in polite company.

CAPITALISM & ITS DISCONTENTS

Things to Do in Evening Shade, Arkansas

So I'm lolling about looking for things to do unlike the things I do every day, including sleeping too late, stuffing myself with foodstuffs, drinking box wine till it comes out my ears, ogling the ladies on the street corners, when I think of Evening Shade, isn't that a lovely name, isn't that the kind of suave and naive place name designed to reassure us in every way, the kind of place or name where you too might like to be buried?

So I'm Googling things to do in Evening Shade, Arkansas, and it turns out there is really nothing to do in Evening Shade, Arkansas except go somewhere else, for example, the Rafter D Ranch, in Mt. Pleasant, where you can ride a horse or book an event space, in case an event is about to happen in your life; or drive north up to Box Hound Marina Resort & RV Park in Horseshoe Bend, where you can rent a pontoon or tube and float down the celestial Spring River; or whack a little white ball around the Turkey Mountain Golf Course, cussing no doubt, at your age, with your skill set; or chow down at Papa Dick's Pizza, also in Horseshoe Bend, which is what it is, Yelp reviewers say, but the staff is so nice, polite, and efficient.

So I'm thinking what kind of beds do they have in Evening Shade, surely someone rents out beds, but Airbnb reveals only a man cave in Cave City, Ms. Tilly's Room at the Historic Hardy Courthouse, and the Street House in Smithville, built in the 1890s, serenely resting only steps away from the banks of picturesque Big Creek.

So how about a place to pitch my tent in Evening Shade? Just a campground or backyard innocent of guile or suspicion of strangers that I might try out, like a final resting place, trying if the ground is comfy, rocky, or just right, somewhere, anywhere for a son of man to lay his head.

4. NEWS OF THE DAY

Supply Chain Resilience

So let's roll up our sleeves, boys, and not rely no
more on 5G chips from Singapore, Taiwan, and China.
Let's build our own plants right here in the star-spangled
USA. The pricey, sophisticated new semiconductors that
power smartphones, video games, and auto components
offer significant potential for broader engagement and
supply chain resilience. Capacity crunch has ripple effects,
and insufficient investment in mature chips, by God and
gory, requiring lengthy revalidation of parts, could cost
us tremendously

NEWS OF THE DAY

Tremors

Rumors of tremors shook our
hillside communities, jogged
memories of ancient declivities:
crocodile gods irate, tsunamis
surging, wailing mothers and
faceless children carried away,
fishermen at sea disappearing.

> With a yawn over French roast
> and croissants, I unfurl the morning's
> *LA Times* and see in Papua New Guinea,
> ho hum, clans clutching hands, looking
> into each other's eyes, washing out
> to sea, corpses bloating.

Thirty-foot water walls shredded our
villages, blasted bamboo and yam.
Matted with mud, reeking of algae,
gods' shrines were overwhelmed.

> Look at the *Eyewitness News,* baby.
> Get a load of the Venice Beach lifeguards,
> ripped and tan, shouting at the lollygaggers
> in the drink, "Get out of the water now!"

Blurred Borders
Science Friday

Scientific research suggests
honeybees distinguish invaders
from nestmates by smell,
chemical signals called CHCs,
cuticular hydrocarbons, cues
from the gut microbial community.

If you change the microbial
biome of a few bees, they
will readily be absorbed
into the hive. But if you
introduce many bee species,
they will attack each other.

If we ourselves could hold
down our proud noses. Or get
inoculated with the same CHCs.
Be readily absorbed into
the common hive, *e pluribus
unum*. You see what I mean?

NEWS OF THE DAY

Base Jump
Men's Journal

>One
of the
best up
and coming
wingsuiters in
the world, Hunt
made his home near
Yosemite, took odd jobs,
flew regularly. By fly I mean
jump off the cliff face into the
void and then sail miles, an exhilar
ating and, admittedly, extreme sport.
On sixteen May, with his mentor Potter,
who called the sport base jumping, Hunt
stepped to the edge of Taft Point, thirty
five hundred feet above Yosemite
Valley, jumped, fell free, veered
hard left to hit the notch they
were aiming for, then hard
right, then hit the moun
tain face hard, I say:
what other kind of
impact could
there be?

LOST & FOUND

First
Hunt, then
Potter. The
spotter, below
in the meadow,
hearing two loud
slams (parachutes
opening? bodies ex
ploding?), tried vainly
to establish radio contact,
then moved to a predetermined
meeting place to see what he could
see. The refreshing thing about Potter,
friends said, was just how unabashedly
himself he was even when pissing off
the National Park Service because
jumping into the void was strictly
illegal, however long men have
longed to fly like birds, with or
without feathers, and when he
slammed into the mountain,
until he was himself no
more, neither shout
nor whisper.

NEWS OF THE DAY

Accidental Elegy

Octogenarian neighbors
swarmed out of trailers
inserting dentures,
mumbling regrets:
he did this to his
sweetheart?

Sure, there were tensions
between 'em, they told the cops,
the usual screaming, hair
pulling, fistfights, so what,
he'd moved out months ago,
and they both doted on their
dainty and rambunctious
daughter, giving her whatever
they could and then some.

Hard to believe he staged
the accident, left her
splayed out in the street
like that, Harley crumpled
and displayed beside her
bloodied body. Guess, said
one old boy, scratching his
bum, whistling through his
choppers, she did just about
everything she set out to do
with him except get old and
everything like that.

Man Charged in Death of Man Found in River

Joel Walter Donovan, 49 years old, was charged in Hennepin County District Court with first- and second-degree man slaughter in connection with the death of a man he was fishing with last week on the Mississippi River.

Arrested several times before for disorderly conduct and assault, Donovan told police he hit Ronald Duncan Wednesday and pushed him onto the rocks along the river, and he also told police he didn't hit or push Ronald Duncan.

Thursday the police found a wet, white, blood-stained T-shirt in Donovan's basement, and Donovan's roommate told them Donovan had said he'd been fishing and had got into a fight and hurt or killed someone.

Donovan told police he had done something "really terrible and felt bad for Mr. Duncan's loved ones," said the police report. Duncan's bruised body was found Thursday in the Mississippi near 10th Avenue and River

Road, the lungs filled with fluid, which likely means he was alive when pushed into the water, according to the Hennepin County morgue, and he'd done something terrible indeed.

5. POLITICS & THE POLITY

Seattle Climate Report

It's hot and dry in Washington,
Greg, over 100 and the forests
going up in smoke. We went
to Alaska for relief and got
sunburn. We are toast. We
did it to ourselves. It's sad
beyond belief. Aren't you
too in distress for the next
generation, and God help
their children.

POLITICS & THE POLITY

Gun Control

The Umpqua Community College killer, "too confused and cowardly to be named," says the sheriff, was enrolled in Writing 115.

Before he began picking off his classmates, producing what they call one more "active shooter situation," he handed over to one of them, "the lucky one," a manifesto of rambling racist resentments and rages and made her watch the massacre.

Whether he was failing or passing the writing class, who knows?

Whether the manifesto contained run-on sentences, subject-verb errors, pronoun-agreement problems, dangling modifiers?

"I've been waiting years to do this," he said, killing his teacher first, Lawrence Levine, 67, of Glide, an avid fisherman and writer, who loved the blues.

"Grandma," the lucky one sobbed, "he killed my teacher."

"The community will pull together," the mayor says.

The shooter was wearing a flak jacket, camo gear, and more ordnance than you would need to annihilate the entire MLA Committee on Community College Best Writing Practices.

He is said to have practiced with his mother at shooting ranges, the two of them toting guns not pens, squinting and taking aim at the obstacles life presented since her divorce from the Englishman.

Kim Saltmarsh Dietz, 59, died at the scene, "a very energetic, very kind, kind soul," according to her ex, who loves her still, "an exceptional woman."

Lucero Alcaraz, 19, died too, who wanted to grow up and help people as a nurse. There is no sense talking about it, his father says, though he says it in Spanish. *"No tiene sentido hablar de eso. ¿Cuál es el sentido de mostrar nuestro dolor?"*

Sarena Dawn Moore, 44, a Seventh-day Adventist, writhing in her wheelchair, was among those shot because she was Christian.

Jason Dale Johnson, 34, also Christian, reassured by the shooter he too would go to heaven, had just begun his first week at school after passing a Salvation Army drug rehab program.

Quinn Glen Cooper, 18, was "funny, sweet, compassionate," a loving person who loved martial arts, dancing, and acting. "Our lives are shattered beyond repair," his family says.

Treven Taylor Anspach, 20, a clerk at a lumber dealer was "one of the most positive people you could ever know."

Chris Harper-Mercer, 26, "too confused and cowardly to be named" but we're naming him anyway, whose armaments included five handguns and one longarm, a virgin, a racist, convinced his "success in Hell is assured," winged by detectives responding to the scene, put a pistol to his head and shot himself.

POLITICS & THE POLITY

Required Reading for Those Who Will Not Read

Dear voter, give it the good old college try, would you, for your sake and the polity? And please kill the TV while you're at it?

Shall we start with Aristotle? Not the *Poetics* but the *Rhetoric*, since you wish to argue things about which you know nothing. Yes, you have pathos up the ass, but what about logos and ethos, my friend, the triumvirate that's ruled disputation since the Greeks? Yes, yes, I know you're 'merican, what are ancient days to you and dead Greeks? Give it a try!

How about the *Oresteia* by Aeschylus? The Greeks knew something about rage and hubris and what to do with 'em: take your enemy's children, cut off their tongues, their balls, doesn't that sound all-American, bake 'em in a pie and serve 'em to the parents.

Yes, throw in the bible if you need it, the sacred text, so and so begat so and so and thou shalt not do this, that, and the other, Exodus, Leviticus, Deuteronomy, eye for eye and tooth for tooth, and the Gospels, milkier and more humane, and then St. Paul, who fell off his horse onto his ass on the way to Damascus, seeing Jesus, who certainly was a Jew, but when he proclaimed himself God that's where I get off the horse and boat. The good book, they say, though gods know there are better (see below).

Skipping centuries and nations, Voltaire's *Candide* is sky-high on the list. What possible interest could you have in a dead Frenchman? Imagine when you are booted out of Trump's castle, Bubba, and must hightail it across the Appalachians fleeing the new Biden administration along with the lady with one buttock, Kamala Harris, who's coming after you with a carving knife, then you'll be glad you know something about the sad, tumultuous human spectacle after all.

How about the English dead? "Whatever I write," John Locke wrote, "as soon as I discover it not to be true, my hand shall be the forwardest to throw it into the fire." Empiricism, or the scientific method. The mind as tabula rasa, not tabor, fife, flag, and dum-dum drum. See *An Essay Concerning Human Understanding*. Edmund Burke argued in *A Vindication of Natural Society* that virtue must be underpinned with manners. So he nixed the Boston Tea Party and French Revolution, and what do you suppose he'd think of MAGA? Edward Gibbon, beginning 1776, took his own sweet time in six volumes and 3,589 pages of *The Decline and Fall of the Roman Empire*. What do you suppose might be the limits of empire?

Listen up, Bubba. For the sake of charity and clarity, let's throw in a few Asians: the Quran, Bhagavad Gita, Analects of Confucius, and the Four Sages.

And a few black folks too, begging your pardon, the 'mericans James Baldwin, Richard Wright, and Toni Morrison. And direct from Africa Chinua Achebe and Bessie Head.

Finally, to add spice and enlightenment, which gods know you could use, the work of women like Mary Wollstonecraft, *Vindication of the Rights of Women* (you've heard of 'em?); Simone de Beauvoir, the shrimp Jean-Paul Sartre's sometime consort, and *The Second Sex;* Sappho, the poetic Lesbian from Lesbos, where else; and Zora Neale Hurston, whose eyes were watching God, and isn't it about time yours were too and not that damned Baptist preacher?

POLITICS & THE POLITY

Homicide Stenographer Rant

According to the police report, a strong odor
of an unknown beverage emanated from her.
She told the cops she'd only had four ginger
beers, though a test revealed a blood alcohol
level of 0.157 percent. Move your fucking car,
you stupid Jew! she'd screamed at the old man,
a fucking Democrat too, though how she knew
who knows, blocking her space in front of Pho
Boca in his white Mercedes-Benz SUV.

Then she backed up her Prius, not a GOP vehicle
you'd think, and smashed the Jew's Mercedes.
I am a Jew myself! she screamed. I am the one
who's getting persecuted! Look how these fucking
Democrats are getting away with murder!

LOST & FOUND

Supreme Court Rejects Trump's Bid to Shield Tax Returns
Reader comments, Washington Post article

Yes, the Witch Hunters are closing in.
The Orange Blob's lifelong crime show
comes to an end. Get your popcorn ready.
He would not last a week on Riker's Island.
What will Spanky McBonespurs' defense be now?
For a good laugh, tune into Carlson or Hannity
tonight. Bad day for Former Guy. Bet he wishes
he'd chosen Stone and Manafort for the court.
Lock him up and throw away the key. A good
last 30 days: Biden president, Limbaugh dead,
and Vance is closing in on Trump's tax records.

POLITICS & THE POLITY

Otto Warmbier: 1994–2017

Poor old Otto Warmbier, funny name, warm
beer, which he might have been drinking in
Pyongyang with that English bloke he took
up with on the tour, the last one who saw him
alive at the airport. Neither old nor funny really,
Otto and his fate. Makes the blood boil, in fact,
doesn't it, to think what Kim Jong-Fuck and
his henchmen did to this twenty-one-year-old
American, stealing a lousy poster of Fatboy,
the Supreme Leader, or trying to steal it,
they said, subversion they called it, a hostile act
against the state, in league with the Methodists,
they charged, and the CIA. Whisked off the flight,
tried in kangaroo court, sentenced to fifteen years'
hard labor, tortured and returned braindead to
the US after 18 months, he died three days later
in a Cincinnati hospital.

Makes you wanna wave the flag, doesn't it? Send
them a bit of shock and awe of our own ... before
we consider KJF's mustard gas, phosgene, sarin,
VX, the new KN-22 ICBM, the fissile material
they produce each year enough for 67 nuclear
warheads, enough madness, theirs and ours,
to destroy the earth several times over.

New York City Climate Report

They lived in a basement
apartment that may or may
not have been strictly legal.
Sure, the forecast called
for rain, but who knew how
much really or just when?

When it rains these days,
however, it pours, and by
the time the three realized
it was a rain event, as they
say, of historic proportions,
three inches in an hour,
Sherpa, Lama, and their
toddler Ang were up to
their necks in water.
The neighbor phoned
and said get out now,
and they replied only
water's coming
in the window.

Next morning Ang's
daycare provider came
to check. "I was afraid
when they didn't call me,"
she sobbed, learning
the entire family had
died hours before. "I
came to see the baby
and the baby died,
everybody died. Oh,
Jesus! The baby and
the parents too!"

6. STORIES REMEMBERED & INVENTED

The Cypriot Way
For Shawn & Kerie

He bade her swim around the black rock
thrice, till she was bushed, beached,
clasped in his arms, and then proposed:
Aphrodite, he said, falling to his knees, will
you marry me? Everything else being as it is,
he suggested, it's not really such a bad deal
after all. I can cook and I can clean, my queen.
The American beauty swooned. He took her
in his arms to the bridal suite. His Cypriot
friends in the street below raised their wine
glasses and shouted huzzah! huzzah! huzzah!

STORIES REMEMBERED & INVENTED

Face 1: Catholic School

It's like Sister Clara said
when I was in sixth grade,
way back in the nineteen
fifties, Mr. Zeck, she said,
wipe that grin off your face,
and I said, Sister, that is
my face, for which wise
crack I beg forgiveness
now how many years later,
for the Lord may suffer
little children to come
unto him, but the nuns
should not have had
to suffer brats gladly.

That kind of life could
not have been easy, all
wimpled up and battened
down to their daily devotions,
up at dawn and down only
at midnight after what kind
of flagellations I don't
dare imagine.

Oh, in fifth grade, I forgot,
Sister Peter (her name, no lie,
and she was seventy if I was a day)
called me her little sunshine
before she intercepted the note
I passed to my best friend saying
meet me on the playground after
lunch for a game of Dr. Dinky
(our pubic hair just beginning

to sprout). You and your
Dr. Dinky! she scolded
us before the entire class.
Bunk! rubbish! fiddlesticks!
nonsense!

We were not her own kids,
I mean, just two squirrelly
boys passing unmindfully
from one grade to the next.

STORIES REMEMBERED & INVENTED

Face 2: Social Media

I get a friend invite from a young face
model in Massachusetts, a young woman
with a pretty enough face, I suppose, to
1) present every day throughout her life
in interactions with friends and family,
amorous relationships, catalogs and ads
and exhibitions, and 2) represent whatever
needs representation — face, from Latin
facia, from *facies,* appearance, which brings
to mind *fasces,* doesn't it, a bundle of rods
with an ax, the blade projecting, shown to
Roman magistrates as an emblem of power,
and what about fascists and the uses of beauty?

Don't rods still compel legions of beauties
with melting face and form, limbs and breasts,
teeth and lips, to march in formation? Or gladly
to kneel before the emperor, whether sneering
duce or multimillionaire, and proclaim they
who are about to die salute the power?

Sure, I'll be your friend, I say. You have
a young, fair face, unlined, two gold hoop
earrings, a white golf cap that says Raptor Bay.
Brown eyes, for sure, brown hair falling
to the shoulders, a frank gaze asking anyone
out there, could be, is there something I can
do for you, or you for me?

Chex

Cognitive capture or, cognitive tunneling, is an inattentional blindness phenomenon in which the observer is too focused on instrumentation, task at hand, internal thought, etc. and not on wider aspects of the present environment. — Psychology Wiki

My townspeople! I cry to the people at the bar. You who once upon a time were my townspeople, who lived next door and we knocked on each other's doors when we needed sugar or a book or a good talk or cry! I knew you or presumed to know you by geographic proximity and neighborly loquacity, gifts of the old days when we looked each other in the eyes and wagged our tongues in each other's faces. Put down those goddamned cellphones now! Let's make good company once more. Let's tell each other about our children, our food, our secret lusts, our politics. Not diddle our days away in the cloud, as they say, our head in the clouds, I say, or up our ass. Let's use our native tongue in communion, shall we, not strangle the muscle electronically or mute it?

So I start throwing Chex Mix into your beers, when one of you, almost my age and old enough to know better, says, with increasing volume and irascibility, "Don't, Greg! Don't! Stop now!" And I say unto him, and you too, brethren, unless we become as little children again, simple and innocent once more, and put down our goddamned cellphones and take up this bread, or these soggy Chex, whichever comes first, that I've vouchsafed unto you, and I'm not the only one that feels this way, feeling the full joy of each other's company, we shall not enter the kingdom of heaven.

STORIES REMEMBERED & INVENTED

Hot Thai Dinner chez Zeck

Kelly comes over and chews some shrooms,
holding them in his mouth as long as possible,
like a lover the first time he kisses a woman
he's been wanting forever or a smack of caviar.
Holly eats the hot Thai take-out and fire pours
from her head, a petite bronze bodhisattva
exhaling Thai food who wants nothing to do
with Thai food. Kelly and I are laughing like
two baboons chewing the shrooms, what do
we want with food at a time like this? Jen's
dish is way hot too, the way she was when
we just met, I could hardly get in the door
without whipping it out and we fell moaning
to the floor while upstairs her parents sat
grazing on *Bonanza*.

Things Our Father Used to Say
Robert E. Zeck, 1913–2008

Smacking his lips, he'd tell Mother, after
dinner, "Thanks for the sumptuous repast."
Always a Catholic gentleman, he would swear
only if severely irked, e.g., "Son of a biscuit!"
If he found you'd copped a feel, he'd say,
"You'd better reexamine your moral principles,"
Or if you desired to marry a minority, "Go right
ahead if you want to ruin your life." And just
once, scaring the pants off my little sister
Jeannie, eight years old or nine, he said,
held up behind a slow woman driver,
"Woman, you dink!"

STORIES REMEMBERED & INVENTED

The Sensitive Zeck Boys

is what my older brother Gerry called us,
quick to take offense, he said, at slights
real or imagined. Slight of build was one
problem, and sleight of hand another.
Sissy! younger brother Bob would tease,
waving his wrist limply. Mama's boy!

It was magical just how slight we were.
When Dad came home we turned sideways,
not wise but invisible. For years we three
hid behind Mom's apron when she baked
the cake and offered us dough-licks.
We took cover beneath her skirts, where
we stayed for years, and even in school,
the first and last refuge of the scoundrel,
we stayed and sauteed, emerging finally
more blue veined and thin skinned the more
we learned and whirled around the earth's
well-beaten bowl.

On a PBS special the other night, a one year
male pachyderm, left behind by matriarch
and herd, was set upon by five young lions,
who ramped up from behind and tried their
teeth on the hide or, biting, licking, mauled
his sides. Nothing they essayed could pierce
the abandoned beast's buttocks. They sank
back exhausted, at last, giving it a break,
and the bull rose up on all fours, trumpeting,
and beat it back into the jungle.

There, for Christ sake, I say to my brothers,
let that be a lesson!

Soul
For Brooks and Linda

So what is the soul?
A casual question
tossed into the mix
of a dinner for four
at the new pizzeria.

Well, you say, your
mouth half stuffed
with creme fraiche
and bacon bits, it's
what's left over after
all this is gone,
gesticulating widely
at the ambiance —
Formica table, liquor
store next door, gas
pumps beyond.

Maybe, you say,
it's the memories,
images, enthusiasms
that have vanished,
you see, fumbling
whilst devouring
your tidbit.

It's what, take away
the body, makes you
you, you try again. So
take away the body,
after all, what's up
and who's who?

STORIES REMEMBERED & INVENTED

It's the horse and
chariot that appear
someday, you say,
sipping your merlot,
to take us away
from all this,
disappearing
like the flame
of the woodfired
oven at day's end
into the empyrean.

But do we really
need Greek any
more? Those left
behind, after all,
may spend their
time, the time
being, chewing,
pointing to the sky
incredulously.

How about it's
the secret of
the cave, way back
there in the dark,
where they keep
the bones?

Or how about
what they taught
you way back when,
the nuns and priests
and ministers: soul is

spirit, they catechized,
bless your eyes, life
force that will never
die, cum understanding
and free will? How
about them apples,
Adam, Eve?

What others under
stand, at any rate,
may be different.
To say nothing
of our long gone
nameless ancestors,
apes and men, as
past results, after
all, are no guarantee
of future earnings.

7. WHEN WE HAVE FEARS THAT WE MAY CEASE TO BE

Fort Riley, Kansas, July 1918
After John M. Barry, The Great Influenza

No letter from my beloved for two days,
no cool days, no cool nights, no drinks,
no movies, no dances, no club, no pretty
women, no shower, no poker, no people,
no fun, no joy, no nothing save heat and
blistering sun and scorching winds and
sweat and dust and thirst and long and
stifling nights and long hours and lone
someness and general hell. That's Fort
Riley, Kansas for you.

WHEN WE HAVE FEARS

To the Sterile Sedge
For Steve Eggers

Perennial herb of fens, your tufty
stems erect and many slender leaves,
your four stalkless spikelets, your
egg-shaped perigynium spreading
or bent backward at maturity, beaked
and double-toothed and dark brown,
your humble nutlet, your staminate-
only, seedless sterility: who will see
you as they speed by on the highway?
They have their own reasons, I suppose,
shopping, meetings, liaisons, work licit
or not on new developments, commercial
or residential, which metastasize and drive
you out, the usual human things that threaten
your species and strengthen ours, for which
we implore your forgiveness and sing this song.

Dunes
After Blake Bailey, Philip Roth: The Biography

No mermaids yet, he reported from Chicago,
with whom to seek conversation, copulation,
cohabitation. Then no afternoons without friends
on Martha's Island, or, needing more privacy,
driving down the coast, screwing in the dunes
and harvesting mussels. If he'd only married
Anna Banana, he might've had a daughter by her
who could take care of him in his old age. If you
ever fuck my daughter, said wife #1, I'll drive
a knife right through your heart. Not only was
he buying cherries in London, married to #2,
he was going bald and would call his mistress
in Connecticut and jerk off, not till he went blind
but came, then hang up. According to his shrink,
his hang-ups included compulsive masturbation,
castration anxiety, narcissism, perfectionism.
So what's not to love or forgive? He put it all
in his own words, after all, thirty-some books,
and kept on trucking until he could no more.

WHEN WE HAVE FEARS

Beautiful Bitches
After Svetlana Alexievich

A friend of mine threw herself under the train.
Is this what you call love? Why did Anna Karenina
do it? I like Western novels better, in which men
shoot themselves over beautiful bitches. I like
successful older men, they're useful. Screw
Solzhenitsyn and his readers who dream of flying.
Power is not reading but knowing how to fly.
When the married millionaire knocked me up,
he would not leave his wife. Today I would flay
him as a hunter flays a wolf. How miserable
to work so hard to keep someone in your life.
You can rent a girl for a night and do things
to her the Marquis de Sade would not dream
of doing. Thousands attend political rallies,
but millions are buying upscale Italian plumbing
fixtures. Being alone is a choice. Really, I'm telling
you nothing. This is all between me and myself.

The Executioner
After Svetlana Alexievich

If you didn't shoot 'em right the first time,
they'd fall down squealing like pigs, vomiting
blood or laughing in your face. Imagine how
unpleasant that would be. At the end of our shifts,
they'd bring us one bucket of vodka, another of
cologne. Blood being pungent as semen, even our
German shepherd would not get near us. Some of
my colleagues, hardy country boys who'd killed
boars, calves, chickens, knew what they were doing.
City slickers, on the other hand, went insane at once.
You had to put the person on his knees, understand,
and shoot him point blank behind the left ear, hear?
At the end of the shift my arm would hang down limp
as a whip, my index finger paralyzed. Shit, it was
a job, like any other, a factory for death, it's true,
and we had our daily quotas.

WHEN WE HAVE FEARS

Shit Bucket
After Svetlana Alexievich

My father was lucky, he survived the war.
My Uncle Vanya, not so much. They sent
him to the coal mines for ten years, and
his wife jumped out a fifth-floor window.
When he came back, he had no teeth, his
hand was withered, his liver enormous.
He went back to work at the same factory,
opposite the man who had turned him in,
and they drank vodka together, read *Pravda,*
attended rallies. Business as usual,
in other words, in the old USSR.

So Vanya insists his son and I have no
idea what it is to be afraid. In the camps
he watched an enormous interrogator stick
a guy's head in a bucket of shit till he drowned.
When uncle's turn came, he gave all the names
he could think of, informed with the best of them,
wouldn't you? He signed everything they put in
front of him, wouldn't you? They dragged him
back to his cell smeared with his own blood,
piss, shit. I don't know, do you, when a person
stops being human?

Tenderness
After Svetlana Alexievich

Russian women, do you crave a little male tenderness?
We are all yours, heroes of the Great Patriotic War,
come back with medals if not arms or legs, no matter.
Invalids they call us, the apparatchiks, shoving us
squealing like pigs into taxis and dumping us
in dilapidated villas far out in the countryside.

Women, do you crave tenderness? So many million
Russian males shot and killed, splattered by machine
guns, blown into bits by mortars, flattened by tanks.
Out here we are gaining weight, cheer, rotundity.
All in all, we are looking pretty good, aren't we?

Come, bring your wheelbarrows and baby buggies,
trundle us along the rutted road toward home.
Take us in your arms, darlings, give us a kiss.
We are such simple trusting creatures, men.
Take us, please. Take us all.

WHEN WE HAVE FEARS

War
After Svetlana Alexievich

Beach season beginning, first berries ripening
and bazaar: wine barrels and cornbread, roasted
chestnuts, cherry plums and pressed tobacco leaves,
hanging cheeses and fresh yogurt, vendors beckoning,
"You don't want it, sweetie, you don't buy it, just
come here and try it." Then gunshots, shoppers
fleeing, young men with Kalashnikovs snatching
women's purses. Old lady and daughter stumbling
away, sack puffing flour. Truck driver sitting
behind steering wheel, white shirt blossoming
blood. A couple in a Lada plowing down the road,
corpse in back. Beside another car, blood puddling.
AK-47 fire, tanks growling, helicopters chack chack
chacking overhead. Keep running. This is war.

8. MESSAGES FROM THE LIVING & THE DEAD

LOST & FOUND

Honest Apology from Christian Girl and Reply
Found on windshield of car at public library parking garage, the message was written on back of business card reading "Arkansas North Chapter, Pilots for Christ, interested in more info or prayer requests call today."

Verso
Hello, I am so sorry,
she writes on the
back of her daddy's
business card, I
accidently [sic]
bumped and scratched
the back of your car.
Feel free to give me
a call and hopefully
[sic] we can get this
thing ironed out.

Recto
I write [hic]:
if you were not
pumping for Jesus,
would you be so
honest or apparently
so, and truly though
a secular humanist
I will feel free and
what's this ironing
out really going
to cost me, a
curious metaphor?

MESSAGES FROM LIVING & DEAD

How Are Things Moving

How are things moving
with you this fine morning,
my brother writes. Mine got
off to a slow start, he declares.
Only three small turds, floaters
all. To be sure, I have slowed down
considerably in this heat, but that's the
family rhythm, as you point out. Now, at
least, I am cooling down and waiting for the
electric inspector to leave my neighbor's drive
way so I can continue, unlicensed, unimpaired,
installing new lights in the garage ceiling. I am a
slow bro, sure, but lucky bro. All I have left to do is
drill one hole in ceiling, feed wire through, catch the
end and attach to receptical, in the sofitt, shit, brother,
I can't spell half-arsed anymore. Must be the bran flakes
I haven't eaten, or was it you who stole them before I woke?

Poem for My Brother in His Own Words

I watch my neighbor's dozen Mexicans digging
out the driveway, packing it with crushed shell,
prepping for stonework. I play with my cat.
I shit two times, shower once, shave once.
I collect rent payments from the USPO, deposit
same in the B of A, drop off my wife's computer
for repair. I organize my hard drive by work
records, eat home-made pizza lunch, watch
doce Mexicans working *otra vez,* download
maps for rental properties, watch dildo mounted
on bike video (needed invention), apply hand
soap to pecker, kiss the cat goodbye and head
for Wachovia Bank to drop off my sweetheart's
signature for a four-point-two-five percent CD,
and I will stop to buy myself an ice cream cone
(chocolate fudge) in Siesta Village before I come
home for another half day of hard work and greasy
sweat and then my pool buddy returns for a dip
with her dipshit husband. Then I make dinner.
Oh, ye gods that art in heaven, so it's said:
now to thaw the sweetmeats.

MESSAGES FROM LIVING & DEAD

The Void
"How Did We Come To Cherish The Void, and Does It Have a Future in Today's Digital World?" — Ellen Lupton

Cherish is the word

that when associated with the word

void

      you might avoid   like the plague

having been taught   to dread it

     but you could be wrong

               it's more you see

      than   the absence

     of an element

    it adds

   balance   separation

          cleanliness   not to

         mention   flow

   you know   it's not **obscene**

unless it's seen that way

by the   egg yolk   in the frypan

of the eye

so cock   your little head   Cock Robin

Charlie Brown   and imbibe

superfruitful

superfluity

the joy   in the leavetaking

spacemaking

as well as coming

into this   not altogether   satisfactory world

it's true

you don't know how many times I've wished that I could hold you

easy for me   to say you might think

am I not the one

who is happily

swirling   the drain

MESSAGES FROM LIVING & DEAD

Squalor
"Wading through the filth we found what we were looking for."
— A fastidious friend

Squalor is a good word, yes, indeed,
squalid as the night was long or his life
was short. *Mon frère Robert* was forty-six:
would you say forty-six was long? Just a chick,
by the way such reckonings may be reckoned
and calculations hatched? What did him in,
you ask, besides the squalid surroundings
with which he surrounded himself? The cat shit
on the carpet, perhaps, nasty enough, the cat
fur that flew when one sat down on the broken
down three legged chair when one dared visit,
the cat piss saturating everything everywhere
one looked and dared not sit, his extensive
pornography collection, one of the finest video
collections of such coarseness in Minnesota,
with titles too rude to mention in a more or less
polite poem like this right up what might be
called his anal sadistic and vainly suffering alley,
may he rest in peace?

Thanks for helping with the expungements,
mon ami, which is to say cleaning up, a thankless
task for which, again, I thank you. Thanks for
going through the *merde* in which we drown,
too many of us, yelping help! help! help! help!
in so many words whilst the lifesaver on the beach,
Mr. Narcissus, blond and beautiful and not a porno
star, is flirting with his girl. No, throw that shit out,
would you? What's worth saving here? Old grocery
bags, receipts, bank statements, loan dunnings,

travel literature to places Bob would never travel
to, neither Wisconsin to escape to, as the license
plates proclaim, nor Manitoba, land of a thousand
sunsets, nor Timbucfuckingtoo, you catch my drift.

Where were we? Standing there, yes, in that cat
stinking room, okay, the newly deceased newly
deceased, the corpus of said deceased bravely
removed by the medical examiners, his corpus
oozing, decomposing in the ninety degree heat
three days seriatim and on the fourth he is arisen
to the morgue. Oh blague! The taste on my tongue
is neither vinegar nor hyssop and certainly no fun.

Give me a sponge mop, pal, a bucket, and some
bleach, and be handy if not a savior. The savor
of the strong beer, the Tusker's, that you bring,
is certainly of comfort and merit. God damn,
we're not gonna settle, this blue law Sunday,
for three two beer. *L'etoile du merde!* We like
it here! What else is new? We'll drink, you and I,
to the recently surceased, who drank his share
and then some. As the ducks say, *mon chère,*
bottoms up and happy fishing!

MESSAGES FROM LIVING & DEAD

Barbara
In the voice of my sister Jeanne Marie

My brother sends me this featherweight parcel
from the prairie. There's no occasion for the gift.
It arrives before spring clears the ground of snow.
It arrives when my soul is heaviest.

Inside I find two small pine cones and a scattering
of leaves from the grave of our sister Barbara,
who died just this last December. In a dream she
came to him, he tells me, bearing a loaf of bread,

hearty and fragrant, a boule she offered the family,
as she was always feeding us — food, jokes, smiles,
stability. The pine cones are not as warm as bread
or our sister's breath and voice, but they will

nourish me, nearly weightless in my palm —
leaves from the autumn past, seeds for new trees.
She does not visit me in daylight or in dreams,
but I carry her lightly in memory

as I carry the pine seeds in my pocket.
My brother alive, though distant in the hills,
my sister, now shade and shadow, together
lift me above the crushing earth.

Robert Goad, 1947–2020
For a Catholic high school classmate I knew only in passing

What was it, finally, did Goad in?
What goaded him to the very end?
Cancer of the pancreas, heart attack?
A smile or a scowl he could never take back?
Forget the mysteries joyful and sorrowful?
Renege on God with just an hour to go?
I pray his passing might be an example
of how to pass on, at any rate, or sample.

MESSAGES FROM LIVING & DEAD

Thomas B. Whitbread, 1931–2016
Died of prostate cancer 1 October 2016

He went to his poetry professor's house
for an hour of opera and when he got there,
the dear old boy was already in his cups,
off his rocker in his rocking chair tearing
out his thinning hair, weeping, crying out
when Jussi Björling, as Rodolfo, sang *sono
un poeta, scrivo, vivo,* and hit high C at
la dolce speranza, holding and amplifying
it, "Did you hear that? Did you hear that?"
Of course, he heard that. That's why folks
paid to come, wasn't it? And then, "Do you
feel accumulations in your thighs?" What
the hell did he know? He was only twenty
one. He wasn't paid to come. A dear old
fellow, certainly, a minor poet and before
long a major friend, a humorous, curious,
and passionate soul who loved trains
and baseball and opera and would not last
forever, and did not, and there you go.

LOST & FOUND

Martin Dworkin, 1927–2014
On learning only years later of the death of someone I had once known in a professional capacity

Preeminent prokaryotic scholar, Professor
Emeritus Marty Dworkin has passed into the realm
of the scientifically unavailable. For many years,
he showed his students how microorganisms come
alive in the lab and in published research. A near
professional musician, this Brooklyn native played
clarinet in klezmer bands and organized a local
chamber music ensemble, the Musical Offering,
for which he would shlump onstage in baggy slacks
and jacket and give erudite off-the-cuff introductions.
Of course, he'd get testy if you questioned irredentist
Israel. He had more than a little authoritarian streak
in him, as I found out first hand, though this can't be
said in an official obit. He loved his dogs, daughters,
grandkids, and wife of 57 years, Nomi (who would
outlive him by three years). On their honeymoon
in Acapulco back in the fifties, he told me, he and his
bride got so sunburned they could not touch each other,
as we cannot touch him now. Prokaryotes, as you may
know, are one-celled organisms without nuclei, the most
primitive and ancient known forms of life, older than Israel
for sure, maybe older than God, their DNA not organized
in chromosomes, the way Marty was organized in lectures,
papers, and books. His specialty was myxobacteria,
soil-dwelling prokaryotes that cluster, fruit, and forage
on just about any living and decaying material available.
Marty will be missed, according to one guest book signer,
in the Myxococcus community.

MESSAGES FROM LIVING & DEAD

Randall Lankford, 1943–2020

By his own inclination and admission,
Randall Lankford is a sorry motherfucker,
not the only one among my friends, to be sure,
nor necessarily the most egregious, but the charge
stands as given. What can I say? He neither writes
nor calls nor undertakes the efforts required to maintain
or shore up friendship. What kind of shit is this? The offices
of friendship require muscle, yes, deliberate maintenance,
hydraulics, we might say, like an old house, aslant on its
foundation, creaking, tottering, the owner peering out
the streaky window anxiously.

On Buzzard's Wings
To be croaked at my funeral

You who dwell in the shelter of the Lord,
who abide in his shadow for life,
say to the Lord:
"My refuge, my rock in whom I trust!"

> And he will raise you up on buzzard's wings,
> bear you up on buzzard's breath,
> allow you to rot like carrion
> and melt in the palm of his hand.

The snare of the fowler will never capture you,
and famine will bring you no fear:
under his wings your refuge,
his faithfulness your shield.

> And he will raise you up on buzzard's wings,
> take you away on swirly thermal things,
> a kettle of vultures do his bidding,
> boiling you in the palm of his hand.

For to his angels he's given a command
to guard you in all of your ways;
upon their hands they will bear you up,
lest you dash your foot against a stone.

> And he will raise you up on buzzard's wings,
> eviscerate the carrion
> till your bones shine like the city on a hill,
> the last true form of faith's bitter pill.

MESSAGES FROM LIVING & DEAD

How Not to Write an Obituary
Write your own before your heirs fuck it up

She passed away peacefully with her children by her side, Jesus appearing in luminous clouds on the other side.

No one cared to see her when she was alive, so they're sure as hell not welcome now.

In lieu of flowers, memorials preferred to Save the Whales, Crickets, Marmots, and Red-eyed Crocodile Skinks.

Perhaps most important of all to Al was educating people on the dangers of holding in their farts. Throughout his long and colorful life, he instructed thousands on the intricate joys of the bum trumpet.

Formerly a resident of Embarrass, he never returned to his home town, and why should he, being a cosmopolitan, not a pig, and avoiding it like the plague it is.

Born in a log cabin, circumcised by his father with a pocket knife, he was well on his way to becoming the next Abraham Lincoln but, alas, was defeated in his first and only electoral contest for municipal dog catcher.

Passed away peacefully after a valorous two-year battle with cancer of the spleen / liver / pancreas / bum / you name it.

Survived by her children and their spouses and a shitload of grandchildren.

He will be sadly missed, or perhaps not, by his children.

One of the town's finest, Herb enjoyed all sports both as player and coach. He loved bright, sunny days, like who doesn't, and the game of golf, about which his wife and kids, let's be frank, didn't give a rat's ass.

Jack was passionate about cars and Indy racing and a great movie buff. In lieu of flowers or poetry, for gods' sakes, see the new James Bond movie.

Used her ticket to heaven, purchased through a career of penance and piety, to join husband George and all her family members.

Passed away peacefully at home, survived by son who loved and cared for her, daughter who betrayed her trust, and miserable grandson who broke her heart.

Hank, a loving husband and father of three, passed away 9/7/2020, age 92, seconds before he was able to tell his children where he hid the family fortune. Too bad he didn't eat more fish. He might have lived a little longer.

She will forever be our own special angel (specify order): Seraph / Cherub / Throne / Dominion / Virtue / Power / Principality / Archangel / Angel.

Passed away from frontal temporal dementia ... and had no more idea, the last three years, than in previous years who her kids or grandkids, coming or going, were.

Went to be with his Lord. Hope he gets along with him better than with his family.

MESSAGES FROM LIVING & DEAD

I've Said All I Have to Say

ENDNOTES

LOST & FOUND

Use these endnotes as a vade mecum if you wish, a quirky guide to help you along the way and supply you with some of the background of the found poems, including their sources.

iii, "Spell to Find a Lost Object." See wishbonix.com/spell-to-find-a-lost-item/.

3, "Frame." By themselves, words often seem unexceptional. They're simply part of the transactive processes of daily life. Give me this, give me that. Please. Thank you. But put in a frame, like that of a poem, they might take on a new life and urgency. In this book, verbal objects lost to our consciousness, or not yet part of it, are found, retrieved, rescued, presented as art. Some of the objects so found and rescued might be analogous to the humble urinal that Marcel Duchamp mounted on a wall at the Armory Show in New York City in 1917; others may have loftier origins and effects.

4, "How to Write a Found Poem." Yes, the dictionary is the chief source here, specifically the Merriam-Webster online dictionary at merriam-webster.com, which features both definitions and etymologies. Words are the history of our travels as a human race, our longings, mergings, conquests, accommodations to other tribes and peoples. So, too, words can be the refuge of the scoundrel found-poet and found-reader.

6, "Sackcloth." My friend Steve Petrini, aka Bembo, like me a Midwest bard, must have said something to me, orally or in writing, about sackcloth. Was it Lent? Was he in a penitential mood? Was he reading Proust again? Or De Sade? At any rate, the impetus of that one word, "sackcloth," spurred me to this ditty. (Why Bembo? In his cups Petrini has been known to fancy himself another Pietro Bembo, Renaissance cardinal and scholar.)

ENDNOTES

7, "Nothing." Petrini made the remark recorded in the epigraph after a visit to his dentist. One thing leading to another, this stray remark led to this poem. Archie, in lines 4–6, is Archibald MacLeish, who wrote the famous modernist meditation "Ars Poetica" in 1928 ("A poem should be palpable and mute / As a globed fruit ... / A poem should not mean / But be.") See poets.org/poem/ars-poetica.

8, "Dung Beetle." I had this conversation, more or less as given, with my friend Gerry Sloan, now retired as music professor from the University of Arkansas. Gerry is a prolific poet and honors me from time to time with the "daily drivel," or poetic output, that he composes on his iPhone.

9, "Rhyme Time." Speaking of ditties, the rhymes in this effort were found in an online rhyming dictionary to which I resort in times of need, or desperation, rhymezone.com. Is rhyme an essential of poetry in the 21st century? Of course not. But it is something that occurs sporadically and irresistibly in just about any language and that the poet can use to accessorize or motorize his verses. In my case, most rhymes are occasional, fortuitous, serendipitous. Here, I hope, they are comical.

10, "Language." Samanta Schweblin is an Argentine novelist. See Alexandra Alter's review "Samanta Schweblin Talks About Her Creepy New Novel," *New York Times,* 30 April 2020 at nytimes.com/2020/04/30/books/samanta-schweblin-little-eyes.html.

11, "Reverie." As this poem suggests, the origin was un- or subconscious. I half-woke one morning with the phrase "improbable ground of essence" running improbably through my head. In the grog of reverie, I bolted out of bed to the computer, Googled the phrase, and found what's given in the first stanza.

12, "Myopia: Word of the Day." This poem was provoked by my wife Jennifer's complaint about clouded vision following cataract surgery. A fortuitous Word of the Day email from Merriam-Webster sent me to the dictionary for more information, and the dictionary, once more, provided insight and solace, though it did not clear up Jen's vision.

13, "Orchidaceous: Word of the Day." Thanks, once more, Merriam-Webster. Thanks, too, to Elizabeth Barret Browning ("How Do I Love Thee?": poets.org/poem/how-do-i-love-thee-sonnet-43) and to my lovely wife Jennifer for being orchidaceous.

14, "Poem Constructed of Words of the Day." This too must have derived from Word of the Day, over the course of several days. The words themselves and the example sentences are from the source, I believe, though I might've manipulated the examples just a bit. The poem was published in the Winter 2021–2022 *Barrow Street* literary magazine.

17, "Bist Du bei Mir." Bach wrote the music to the verses of this famous song. He seems to have found the lyrics in the opera *Diomedes* by a musical contemporary named Gottfried Heinrich Stölzel (en.wikipedia.org/wiki/Bist_du_bei_mir.) Who the poet was, who knows? In line 5, *Bübchen* means boy (bubby, Bubba) and *Mädchen* girl (maiden).

18, "Jazz Allegro." John Milton wrote the companion poems "L'Allegro" (the cheerful person) and "Il Penseroso" (the contemplative or thinking person) to debate different lifestyles and sources of poetic inspiration. Euphrosyne, line 11, is the

ENDNOTES

spirit of gladness and cheer in "L'Allegro." See romantic-circles.org/editions/mws/lastman/milton.htm. Milton served as a secretary to Oliver Cromwell, the Puritan leader, in the 1650s, the interregnum between the overthrow of the first Stuart kings and their Restoration. As for the voice in the poem, it's "cultural expropriation" for sure, both black and white, integrating a couple of very different strains, a bit of seventeenth century Puritan English and mid-twentieth century jazz: thus, the tension between the ideas of jazz and Milton's poetry. Yes, I'm all for culture as expropriation — bits and pieces lost and found and swapped round and round, juices changed and exchanged. But what do I know, right? I didn't start this fight.

19, "Miller's Tale." In Geoffrey Chaucer's "Miller's Tale," from the *Canterbury Tales,* an old man marries a young woman, Alison, but can't keep scholarly, clever, and horny youths away from her. One of them professes his love for her in pastoral terms (last stanza). The French *jeune fille* means young girl or maiden. The French in the last line refers to a 1960s protest against *medicalizing psychiatry,* which analyzes, judges, and condemns mentally challenged individuals, shall we say, according to moral and authoritarian norms. You might know the name of the social commentator and philosopher Michel Foucault in this context. The poet in this poem expresses disdain for easy moralistic judgment.

20, "Poem I've Been Hoarding in a Drawer." The American poet Frank O'Hara, 1926–1966, was known for his anti-academic free verse; at his death, many poems he'd dashed off were found in his chest of drawers. Or so I seem to recall. Vocabulary: *sere* is a rather archaic word for dry; *spraints* = otter shit; and *anoesis* = primal physiological cognition without trace of rationality.

21, "Tempus Fugit." Everyone with a little Latin knows that *tempus fugit* means time flies. (As a Catholic boy in the 1950s and '60s, I had more than a little church Latin. Catholics then used a missal during mass with Latin on the left side of the page and the vulgate on the right.) The next short, vulgar English sentence ("Fuck it") is known, if not acknowledged or used, by all English speakers. In Latin you might call this poem a *carpe diem* (seize the day) exercise, a defiance of time and bid to make good use of what is left. The poem arose somehow after a short visit to Northwest Arkansas, during the Covid pandemic, from ex-sister-in-law, Pam Tuke Zeck, who suffers from MS and bears it bravely, and her boyfriend Mike Kern. Pam was so good as to bring along several of her superb modern quilt hangings and to sell a couple at family discount. Her art too defies time and the seasons, shaking its pretty fist, sticking out its tongue, and saying, "Bah, sir, I spit on you!"

22, "What We're Looking For." These are statements, taken nearly verbatim, believe it or don't, from editors at little literary magazines throughout the country. Despite these politically charged and tone-deaf declarations, writers throw their manuscripts over the transom and hope they land on heads more sensible than these declarations would suggest.

24, "Refugees." I wrote this poem, an exercise in collective memory, after reading Bao Phi's poem "Adrift" (poets.org/poem/adrift). My dad's family of Polish farmers entered the US via Galveston in the 1870s. They made their way up the Mississippi not too long afterwards and settled on farms near St. Cloud, northwest of the Twin Cities. Some of them, including my dad's dad, couldn't wait to get off the farm.

26, "April Fool's Day Hike." If you're as old as I am, you remember the Beatles and their wacky song "Come Together,"

ENDNOTES

which "was composed for Timothy Leary's campaign to stand against Ronald Reagan as governor of California," according to beatlesbible.com/songs/come-together. Another source says that this John Lennon "song topped the charts in the United States and became an anthem of sorts for the anti-war movement (gizmodo.com/john-lennon-wrote-come-together-for-timothy-leary-but-1618446177). My poem came together after I led a group of hikers in Hobbs State Park, in Northwest Arkansas, spring of 2020, and was bitten by a lone star tick. This insect injects alpha gal into its victims, a protein native to most mammals but not man. Once injected and infected, humans can have allergic reactions ranging from mild to fatal when they eat, or even smell, mammal meat. I had Alpha Gal Syndrome, or AGS (mayoclinic.org/diseases-conditions/alpha-gal-syndrome/ symptoms-causes/ syc-20428608), for a year or so but luckily went into remission and was able to resume the life of a red-blooded carnivore. In the interval, I ate a lot of chicken, fish, duck, and emu. (Thanks for bearing with me, Jennifer, and cooking so creatively under the circumstances.)

27, "Waldeinsamkeit." Seems to me, in the mists of memory, that when I was an undergraduate at the University of Minnesota and then grad student at UT Austin, taking German literature classes, I read in many Romantic texts about *Waldeinsamkeit* (literally, the loneliness or solitude of the woods). The text cited here is the story of Hansel and Gretel from the Grimm Brothers. This poem melds a memory of language learning with a recent experience, when I went out to hike the woods solo and found myself, what else, lost ... while daylight was fading rapidly.

31, "Men's Health." Where do they get this stuff, the publishers of *Men's Health* and other such supposedly health-oriented magazines? Their audience does not include too many poets or philosophers, I trust.

32, "Enlarge Your Penis Now." I must've picked up these fantasies from the Internet, yes? Google the title phrase and you'll find more than you bargained for. Don't blame me!

33, "Pahokee, Florida." Yes, I believe there is a Podunk place called Pahokee. At least, I got a junk phone call from the place and so began this celebration.

34, "Poem in Two Faces and Seven Fonts." My dad, Robert E. Zeck, was a lawyer, and he let me practice on one or another of his manual typewriters when I was an ornery adolescent learning the typing trade. This standard practice sentence ("Now is the time ...") was one of Dad's favorites. Thanks for the memories.

35, "James Patterson Teaches How to Write a Best-selling Novel." The ad for this online course appeared in my junk email folder one day, and somehow I found it and fished it out. The rest, as they say, is history. I'm afraid I will never write a good novel, even a good formula novel, though I have tried. Poetry is enough of a challenge and something I apparently can do.

36, "Out of Sorts and Out of Work." Must've been such an actual ad for a "failure analysis technician" that I espied, somewhere, sometime, and I responded in the form of this poem.

37, "Principal Life." This text conflates a Globe Life ad and a couple of stories from my life. Globe Life Inc. bombards prospects with magazine ads and email solicitations, as you

ENDNOTES

may know. Back in the '70s, when I was teaching in Detroit, my wife Jen and I had a couple of insurance agents. One was the cousin of my sister-in-law Pam Tuke; he would preface every sales pitch, which was also a memento mori, with the phrase "God forbid something should happen to you, Greg." The other agent was my sister Jan's husband John McCarthy, a damned fine man and may he rest in peace; when Jen and I lived in Detroit, we would make holiday visits to our folks in the Twin Cities, sometimes stopping in transit in Green Bay, where John sold insurance for Principal and others. One day he regaled us in his office with an audiovisual sales pitch that deployed out of a briefcase. The tone of the presentation was old-fashioned and melodramatic, as if produced in the 1950s, and before long Jen and I were laughing so hard we were crying. What can I say? We signed the new life insurance policy on the dotted line. Oh, in the 1980s Jennifer worked in Minneapolis for Principal, whose name has a suggestive ring here.

38–39, Product Reviews. These poems come almost verbatim from Amazon customer reviews, with grammar, spelling, and logic intact. The people have spoke!

40–42, Wine Reviews. These reviews too were found online, with few changes except selection and condensation and the memorable phrase "Corpulent and chewy," which comes not from the Matsu el Recio review but a shelf tag found at a liquor store near our house in St. Paul, Minnesota about 1990. The name of the wine escapes me.

43, "Search Me: LinkedIn." Yes, Linked-In, another social medium, is more than happy to correspond with you, or jam emails down your gullet, as many times per week as you can bear. It sent me a notice recently saying I had just one measly

LOST & FOUND

search on my name that week. I no longer use Linked-In for business, since I retired, and never paid the fee for the premium version, which would unlock the names of those who were searching me.

44, "Things to Do in Evening Shade, Arkansas." As the text suggests, the source is Google and other computer search functions. Inspired by the name Evening Shade, a place I knew in passing (or passing through) from the days of visiting my parents in retirement in Cherokee Village in north central Arkansas, I Googled "Evening Shade" and came up with the notions suggested here. As for "a son of man," at the end, note it's not "the son of man."

47, "Supply Chain Resilience." By late 2021 we are tired to death of all the talk about the supply chain. This poem derives from a spring 2021 article in the *Washington Post* about a shortage of silicon chips for autos (washingtonpost.com/technology/2021/03/01/semiconductor-shortage-halts-auto-factories/). What struck me about the article was its rah-rah business quotes and its completely uncritical use of business jargon, as if the reporter lacks time, as well as inclination, to correct or challenge language like "supply chain resilience," "capacity crunch," and "mature chips"; but imagine living uncritically under the big top of this linguistic nonsense. Better, perhaps, we not demand anything from overseas, but read poetry, which is not locked up in containers on the seas or docks.

48, "Tremors." Which tsunami was this and just when? Might have been the Boxing Day Tsunami of 2004 or the 2011 tsunami that destroyed the Fukushima nuclear reactor in Japan. At any rate, news of this dread event reached the comfy

ENDNOTES

USA but did not wash us out to sea. We yawned in our beds, ate our tidbits, and turned the page.

49, "Blurred Borders." Occasionally I find myself listening, lazy Friday afternoons, to the NPR show "Science Friday." On this particular Friday, 23 April 2021, I was struck by a story about bees and their microbiomes and imagined a parallel between the living arrangements of their species and ours. I also consulted a few articles like "'Honey Bee, It's Me' — Gut Bacteria Is [sic] Key to Bee ID" (scitechdaily.com/honey-bee-its-me-gut-bacteria-is-key-to-bee-id/), which suggests, "Increasingly a topic of research interest, the microbiome, scientists have discovered, in many ways blurs the borders between a host and its bacteria."

50, "Base Jump." This poem derives from *Men's Journal,* May 2015, an excellent article about the bravery, foolishness, and fragility of man. And maybe man only, for when I read an earlier version of the text to an audience of other writers, mainly women, they unanimously judged the men referenced here to be idiots. It was some time later that I turned earlier versions of the verbal exploration into concrete poetry with a wingsuit shape.

52, "Accidental Elegy." I'm sure this story came from a newspaper account way back when, but at my age I can't imagine just where and when.

53, "Man Charged in Death of Man Found in River." This story can be found in the *St. Paul Pioneer Press,* 27 April 1999, by Rachel E. Stassen-Berger, who since that day has gone on to report, and edit, for the *Star Tribune* and the *Des Moines Register.*

57, "Seattle Climate Report." This is an almost verbatim transcription of a text message I received, the hot dry summer of 2021, from my friend Sujoy in Seattle, who had lived in Northwest Arkansas until recently and whose very bright son Sohan I used to tutor. How can you say it more simply and more affectingly than this?

58, "Gun Control." This catalog poem is based on a newspaper account of just one of the many horrific mass killings in this gun-crazy country. The Oregon event occurred 1 October 2015.

60, "Required Reading for Those Who Will Not Read." The stimulus for this piece was the entire presidential election cycle of 2020, which began well before 2020 and has not died down yet, what with the January 6 investigation and the CDC's Covid vaccination campaign. "You can't teach those people," my wife has said. Some people (those *other* people, of course) will not be taught (by us), having a fraught history with teachers, could be, and will not learn except on their own, largely corporeal terms. Obviously, there is a connection between critical reading and credulity.

62, "Homicide Stenographer Rant." This tirade comes from an account in the *Washington Post,* 3 February 2021. The ranter proved to be a retired stenographer for the Miami-Dade police homicide division.

63, "Supreme Court Rejects Trump's Bid to Shield Tax Returns." This poem was found in reader comments on a *Washington Post* article of this title published 22 February 2021. I love to hear the wisdom of literate people applied to politics, at least the politics I favor.

ENDNOTES

64, "Otto Warmbier: 1994–2017." News-conscious adults will remember this awful story, which reminds us of the delicate position of democracy in a world of brutal dictators.

65, "New York City Climate Report." This poem derives from a poignant account of the deaths of people in New York City and nearby as a result of a "savage storm" induced by climate change. See https://www.nytimes.com/2021/09/02/nyregion/nyc-flooding-deaths.html.

69, "The Cypriot Way." This story was told by my neighbors Shawn and Kerie Allen, who were visiting friends in Cyprus some years ago, when Shawn, a Fayetteville police officer, had his fiancée Kerie swim three times around Aphrodite's Rock, a ritual to guarantee eternal beauty, as Aphrodite was supposed to have been born on this spot. For more on Aphrodite's Rock, or Petra Tou Romiou (Rock of the Roman), see en.wikipedia.org/wiki/Petra_tou_Romiou.

70–72, "Face 1: Catholic School" and "Face 2: Social Media." The first face poem is a memory of Catholic grade school, the second of a recent social media transaction on LinkedIn. Like other poems in this collection, the social media poem whips up a bit of etymological and lexical froth.

73, "Chex." A true story, more or less, that happened one night two or three years ago when I joined a group of friends at a bar. The idea of addressing people as "townspeople" comes from William Carlos Williams' great poem "Tract" (poetryfoundation.org/poems/45503/tract), in which he instructs fellow citizens how to celebrate a funeral (with joy, not sour faces). Don't you think civility, and joy too, might be restored by banishing cell phones on social occasions? The epigraph can be found at psychology.wikia.org/wiki/ Cognitive_ capture.

74, "Hot Thai Dinner chez Zeck." This dinner occurred not long ago at Jen's and my house in Fayetteville. We invited friends, had a few drinks and chews, then ordered Thai take-out, at which point the night got hot.

75, "Things Our Father Used to Say." The "our father" of the title is here my father if not yours. Dad was a firm believer in "moral principles," as recorded here. He was a "Catholic gentleman" and certainly belonged to "the old school," as he used to say of his own father Tony Szczech.

76, "The Sensitive Zeck Boys." I remember the occasion when my older brother Gerry spit out this phrase, like a preacher denouncing sin, as if at the tender age of 65 or 70 the idea had just occurred to him. The three Zeck boys — Gerry, Greg, and Bob in chronological order — had always been sensitive, as recounted or reflected here. Now there's only one of us left, and he's become something of a pachyderm himself, though he's beat it only to the Ozarks of Northwest Arkansas not the jungle.

77, "Soul." A couple of years ago Jen and I went out to a new pizza joint with our friends Brooks Garner and Linda Leavell, both retired professors from Oklahoma State University. Brooks must have been reading philosophy or religion, for he began speculating, even before the pizza popped out of the oven, about the nature and origins of the soul.

83, "Fort Riley, Kansas, July 1918." Based on John M. Barry, *The Great Influenza: The Story of the Deadliest Pandemic in History* (2004), these words belong almost verbatim to Capt.

ENDNOTES

Francis Blake, writing to his wife from the desolate confines of Ft. Riley, Kansas during the run-up to the Spanish flu. Thanks, John M. Barry, for quoting and acknowledging this in your fine history of the Spanish flu, which began, as you make clear, in Kansas, USA, not in Spain. Barry's book predates and even presages the coronavirus pandemic of 2019 and beyond, but since when do we sit up and take notice when doom is fast approaching?

84, "To the Sterile Sedge." This botanical tribute I took from *Wetland Plants and Plant Communities of Minnesota and Wisconsin* (usace.contentdm.oclc.org/digital/collection/p266001coll1/id/2845), co-authored by Steve Eggers of the Army Corps of Engineers, whom I once interviewed for an article on calcareous fens for my client, the Lower Minnesota River Watershed District. Without getting pious or obvious about it, we can say that man's disruption and destruction of the environment is one more cause of moral and mortal concern these days.

85, "Dunes." Words and ideas here are taken from various portions of Blake Bailey's *Philip Roth: The Biography* (2021).

86–90, Svetlana Alexievich. These five poems owe to the astonishing words and stories of the Nobel Prize winner Svetlana Alexievich's oral history *Secondhand Time: The Last of the Soviets*. Almost every page of the volume bristles with Doestoevskian stories of WW II (the Great Patriotic War), the Khrushchev years, and especially the breakup of the Soviet Union under Gorbachev and Yeltsin. The stories are so dramatic, painful, heartrending they make you almost ashamed to be a safe, secure bourgeois.

93, "Honest Apology from Christian Girl and Reply." I was using the Fayetteville Public Library recently, a much larger facility than you'd expect in a city of 72,000 (2010 census), and when I returned to the car in the parking garage I found the note given in the first part of the poem, "Verso." It was printed in a square girlish script on the back of a business card that read "Arkansas North Chapter, Pilots for Christ, interested in more info or prayer requests call today." The rest, as they say, is history.

94, "How Are Things Moving." This is one of several poems depending on brother Gerry's emails. He was an accomplished cartographer, photographer, illustrator, mythmaker, and poet, though his poetry did not come in the shape of verse lines. His emails, almost always keenly perceptive and funny, were poems in their own right. Yes, I was a lucky bro to have a lucky bro like him, loaned as brother during his lifetime (1939-2016). In this epistolary poem, he seems to be waiting behind a curtain for the authorities to depart and leave him up to his own devices, which like mine were not always strictly legal.

95, "Poem for My Brother in His Own Words." These once more are the words of brother Gerry, who though not required to punch a clock makes a nice account of his day. In fact, Gerry hated punching a clock and like me was often gainfully unemployed.

96, "The Void." See "An Ode to White Space" by Ellen Lupton in *Ambidextrous* (issuu.com/ambidextrousmag/docs/ issue11.) Though Ms. Lupton's article is about white space in graphic design, I extend the idea here.

98, "Squalor." This poem is about my younger brother, Bob (Robert M. Zeck), 1949-1995. I have written quite a few poems

ENDNOTES

about him (see my first volume of poetry, *Transitions*). We were just 15 months apart and had one of those love-hate relationships that are endemic to siblings too close together. When he died, of alcoholism, I had 2-3 friends drop into his squalid apartment and help me clean it out.

100, "Barbara." This tribute poem started with a draft of a poem my little sister Jeannie sent me some time ago and on which we then collaborated. Like older brother Gerry and me, she has a Ph.D. (hers, like mine, in American lit) but more sense and tenderness. Our oldest sibling, Barbara Murphy, died at age 74 in December 2009, within a year of her husband Russell's death. The oldest of seven children, she was a second mother to her siblings, a devout and funny and lovely woman whom we all miss terribly.

101-104, In Memoriam. These poems are tributes or reflections about men I once knew, if only a little, now beyond reach and clarification. Mr. Goad, sorry about the pun on your name, but how can I resist? You were tall and bright, smiling and crewcut, and I knew you only from a few high school reunions. Thomas Bacon Whitbread, dear professor friend, you were full of comedy, eros, enthusiasm, and, yes, when you sang *Lieder* with me and Jen, who played the piano, when we were first married, in Austin, Texas, and you came to dinner, you fairly spit out Schubert and Schumann. Marty Dworkin, head of the M.D./Ph.D. program at the University of Minnesota, I wrote and designed a recruitment brochure for your program and then fliers and a website for the chamber music ensemble, the Musical Offering, that you headed. Randall Lankford, you did in fact write me a letter much like the opening of this poem, but, modest fellow that you always were and unduly apologetic, you were not in fact one of the friends who neglected me in the manner you described; Jen and I met you in Mexico about 1990, when you had just quit North Carolina and the States for good. You were a wonderful, lively, humorous, bilingual friend and died of cancer, quickly, and without recourse to the hospital, in May 2020.

105, "On Buzzard's Wings." Fr. Michael Joncas and I get wiggy on this duet or counterpoint. Fr. Michael is the author of the devotional hymn "On Eagle's Wings," quoted in the unindented stanzas. Fr. Greg (well, I did study one year for the priesthood, way back in ninth grade, in a seminary in Ohio) is now a secular humanist who, every time he steps out the door of his home in Northwest Arkansas, is liable to see a kettle of turkey vultures circling overhead. "Ain't dead yet!" he exclaims, scurrying back inside.

106, "How Not to Write an Obituary." For morbid or comorbid reasons, I've been collecting obits for years. Some are hilarious and many pitiful. At any rate, I present these far-out if not in-deep specimens for your delectation and guidance. Study these examples, please, and forbid your heirs to write such stuff. Flee from the wrath and embarrassment to come: write your own obit now.

108, "I've Said All I Have to Say." Not really, but this book has to end somewhere, doesn't it, and I'm exhausted. Thanks for reading. I appreciate your kind attentions.

GRAPHICS

Cover art with permission of Judy McSween, painter and grade school teacher in North Carolina. I found the basis for the cover art on Pinterest, where Ms. McSween says, "I save gently used socks, mittens, and gloves for our puppet center. (It's a great way to recycle those single items when one of the pair gets lost!) I love this glove puppet a third grader made" (Pinterest.com/FamiliarAbstract Painter/).

You can find Ms. McSween's own artwork on her website at judymcsween.com/home.html.

For the cover of this book, I colored and modified Ms. McSween's puppet in Corel PaintShopPro.

The book typography, design, and layout I did myself.

Author photo on next page was taken by my spouse Jennifer Zeck on the occasion of our 50th wedding anniversary, 19 December 2020.

BIOGRAPHY

Greg Zeck was born in Milwaukee in 1947 and grew up in the Twin Cities. With bachelor's and doctor's degrees from the universities of Minnesota and Texas, respectively, he taught college writing and literature in the Midwest and, one year, in Serbia as a Fulbright lecturer. Along with teaching, Greg also headed a business communications consultancy. Since 1970 he's been married to Jennifer Saltzman Zeck. In 2011 they retired and moved from Minnesota to Fayetteville, Arkansas, following in the footsteps of their son Gabriel, daughter-in-law Heidi, and granddaughter Ruby. *Lost & Found* is Greg's second book of poetry, following one year after *Transitions: Early Poems, 1979–1989*. For more about Greg, including contact information, go to www.youngzeck.com.

www.ingramcontent.com/pod-product-compliance
Lightning Source LLC
Chambersburg PA
CBHW022106040426
42451CB00007B/145